HOW TO BE
HAPPY
FOR EVER

No, really!! :)

Everlasting peace and joy through the prayer Jesus taught

———————————

DAVID C. MITCHELL

CAMPBELL
PUBLISHERS
GLASGOW SCOTLAND

CampbellPublishers.com

Copyright © 2023 David C. Mitchell

Brightmorningstar.org

Illustrations, J.J. Tissot

The author has asserted his moral right under the Copyright, Designs and Patents Act, 1988, to be identified as the author of this work

First Edition

978-1-916619-01-2

*For the Nurses, Doctors, and Orderlies of Ward 29
in the Royal Alexandra Hospital, Paisley*

Contents

1. One Little Thing

THERE'S ONE little thing you can do that will turn your life around and make the sun shine on all your ways.

This little thing is such a big thing that it will make you happy for ever.

Happier than zumba or yoga.

Happier than sunbathing or greenbathing.

Happier than Tai Chi or Qigong.

Happier than squats and pushups.

Happier than Belgian chocolate and waffles.

Happier than Copacabana or Ipanema.

Happier than a Jackie Chan movie.

All these things are great in their place. But this one thing is better.

Unlike some of these other things, this one simple thing won't cost you anything. Not a cent. Not a penny. Not a single solitary centime. Nada.

What's more, it won't take much of your time. Only about thirty seconds a day.

But these thirty seconds will ignite within you a powerhouse that will transform your life and bless the world around you.

I wrote this book to share this secret with you. So I guess I shouldn't keep it up my sleeve any longer.

The secret of *How To Be Happy For Ever* lies in the prayer that Jesus taught. Some folk call it the Lord's Prayer. Others call it the Our Father.

In this book, I am saying something dead simple. It's this. Say this prayer – the Our Father, the Lord's Prayer – every day, and it will open to you the road to happiness here and forever. You can start now.

> *Our Father who art in heaven,*
> *Hallowed be thy name,*
> *Thy kingdom come,*
> *Thy will be done in earth as it is in heaven.*
> *Give us this day our daily bread,*
> *And forgive us our debts*
>   *as we forgive our debtors,*
> *And lead us not into temptation,*
> *But deliver us from evil.*
> *For thine is the kingdom, the power, and the glory,*
>   *for ever and ever. Amen.*[1]

Said it? Good. You've put the first foot on the road to turning your life around. In the following chapters I'll tell you a bit more. I'll show how and why the Our Father can turn your life around in this way. I'll show what you can do to assist the process. But the main thing for now is just to keep saying these words every day.

After you've read the book, you can pass it on to someone else to turn their life around too. Or get them a copy of their own. That's why there's a panel on the front page saying "A Gift For..." Fill in that panel for your sister, your uncle, your mother, your son, your pal. For anyone you feel needs a blessing in his or her life.

But of course you should read it for yourself too. For this little book will tell you what the Our Father can do for *you*. It's not a theological commentary or a philosophical treatise. It's a how-to book to make you happy.

You see, I suspect you are asking the question, "What can make my life happy?" Or, "How can I prosper and progress and do well in my life?" Most folk ask such questions. So I imagine you may be asking them too. And they are very good questions to ask. And that's why, in every little chapter of this book, I will show how this little prayer can answer these questions. How it really can make your life happier. Today. And tomorrow. And the day after.

Maybe you think the Lord's Prayer is a Sunday thing. It's not something you say at home. But I tell you that it's as important as breathing. If you really want to live, you can't do without it.

I don't claim to be a total expert. No one is a total expert on prayer, especially not on this prayer. We are all beginners.

But there's an old saying, "Those who pray, prosper." And, believe me, those who pray this prayer prosper most of all. And in this book I'll explain why.

This book is based on my own experience. What I say here has made me happy. And I promise that if you do what this book says, then you will be happy too. For ever.

It has thirty chapters and a conclusion. So if you read one chapter a day, you can pretty much read it in a month. (Unless, of course, you start in February.) Then say the Lord's Prayer after each chapter.

So begin today. Just say the Our Father, word for word, for a month. After a month, you can decide how your life is looking. If it's looking better, then maybe you'll know why.

2. The Land O' The Leal

THIS BOOK is dedicated to the medics of a hospital in Paisley, Scotland. In that hospital, in January this year, my old mother died.

The doctor had told her, in summer 2022, that she had cancer. He gave her a year to live. But the cancer spread quickly in her body. Soon she had continual pain in her back and couldn't swallow.

In December, she had a fall. She was taken into hospital. She couldn't walk or eat. They asked if she wanted to be fed by a tube in her throat. She said no, and asked them not to prolong her life. So, over five days, she died, mostly of dehydration.

We talked with her about her death. She had no fear. But she said, "I didn't want it to be like this. Not alone in a hospital. I wanted to die at home."

We talked with the hospital staff. An easy death, they said, would need constant oxygen, constant regulation of morphine, constant turning and care. Such a level of care would not be possible at home.

So it was in hospital that she had to die. But we didn't let her die alone. Through her last days, we sat with her by day and slept by her at night. Her last words to me were, "I love you very much." Then, not long after, she was gone.

I gave the tribute at her funeral. I quoted a Scots song called *The Land o' the Leal*. ("Leal" is an old Scots word for "loyal" or "faithful".) In the song, a lady is dying and she tells her husband:

> *I'm wearin' awa', John,*
> *Like snaw wreaths in thaw, John,*
> *I'm wearin' awa' tae the Land o' the Leal;*
> *There's nae sorrow there, John,*
> *There's neither cauld nor care, John,*
> *The day is aye fair in the Land o' the Leal.*[2]

My mother was leal. She was leal to her family, leal to her friends, leal to her church, leal to everyone. She stuck by her commitments and didn't let folk down. Above all, she was leal to Jesus, leal to her Bible, leal in prayer.

She became a believer in the Lord Jesus in her early teens. Her family were members of the local Church of Scotland which had a thriving youth group. The minister thought that this was thanks to his great preaching. But, said my mother, it was all due to the janitor, wee Bobby Gallagher. He went round all the kids asking, "Are ye saved yet? Are ye saved yet?"

So my mother got saved too and lived her life before the Lord. In her early twenties, she thought she might become a missionary. But then my father appeared and swept her off her feet. So she lived happily in a little town in the west of Scotland.

In that life, she blessed thousands of people –

within her family, right down to her great-grand-children, in her work as a primary school teacher, in her part in local churches and choirs. She joined the Glasgow Cooperative choir at the age of seven and was a keen choral singer for as long as she had a voice. She read her Bible every day. (Her Bible was worn out.) She was a major influence on my love for the Bible and all kinds of church music.

Although we missed her when she left, we were happy rather than sad. For she couldn't stay. Her body was crumbling and she was in constant pain.

In the last part of the *The Land o' the Leal*, the dying lady tells her husband that they will be happy for ever in the Land o' the Leal.

> *So dry your tearfu' e'en, John,*
> *This warld's cares are vain, John,*
> *We'll meet and aye be fain in the Land o' the Leal.*[3]

We know that my mother has gone to the Land o' the Leal where there's no sorrow. She's gone to meet the Lord Jesus whom she loved. We know that one day we'll meet again. We know that together we'll all be happy for ever.

There's another old Scottish song, a Christmas carol called "Child in the manger." It ends like this.

> *Prophets foretold him, Infant of wonder,*
> *Angels behold him on his throne;*
> *Worthy our Saviour of all their praises;*
> *Happy for ever are his own.*[4]

Everyone who loves the Lord Jesus will be happy for ever. Some die in peace, others in war. Some die in honour, others in dishonour. Some die at home, others in hospital, which is not what they wanted. But all will be happy for ever.

I cannot thank and praise highly enough the dedication and care of the nursing staff in the Royal Alexandra Hospital in Paisley. They cared for my mother while other NHS staff around the country were on strike. (Not that the Ward 29 nurses were unsympathetic to the strike. They explained to me just how much they are understaffed and under-resourced.)

One young nurse there had her own sorrows. Her mother had died during the COVID pandemic of 2020. Because of the quarantine imposed during the COVID lockdown, she could not even sit with her mother as she lay dying.

All the nurses were great. But this young lady cared for my mother with unexpected compassion. She offered us her sympathies with tears in her eyes when my mother finally died.

When it was all over, I wanted to do something to thank them. I bought them some big tins of best Scottish shortbread. But I wanted to do something more. Something to make them happy for ever. I'd already been thinking a lot about the Lord's Prayer. So that's when I decided to write this book for the nurses and medical staff of Ward 29.

3. Happy For Ever?

THIS BOOK is about how to be happy for ever. Maybe you think that's a crazy fairy-tale. Like, please! Who still believes in a Happy-Ever-After?

Well, I do. But it's not from the Fairy Godmother. It's from higher up.

Maybe you think this is impossible. Or maybe you think it's impossible for you. But read on. There is a way to be happy for ever, even for you.

In 1955, that grand old American preacher, Billy Graham, wrote a book called *The Secret of Happiness*. It's a great book. But this book in your hand is a bit different.

For a start, Billy Graham's book is based on Jesus's words in the Beatitudes – *Blessed are the poor in spirit* – from the Sermon on the Mount (Matt. 5:3–12). But this book in your hand is based on the Lord's Prayer. The Lord's Prayer is from the same Sermon on the Mount (Matt. 6:9–13). But it's even more basic to Christian faith than the Beatitudes. I'll tell you why in a moment.

What's more, back in the 1950s, folk lived closer to faith. Billy Graham kind of assumes his readers already have one foot on the ladder of faith.

But not everyone has. So this book is designed for folk who don't have a foot on the ladder. Folk who don't always get it right. Folk who don't know the rules. Folk who can't make ends meet. Folk with mess-up lives. Those with bad habits. Those who've been mistreated. Those who can't get on for falling off. Those whose lives aren't straight, but broken. People not on the ladder. People lying in the dirt a hundred miles from the bottom of the ladder.

One more thing. Billy Graham's book is all about doing. He says that if you live the kind of lifestyle painted in the Beatitudes, then you'll be happy.

But I say, living that lifestyle is really hard. None of us can really manage it properly. We can try. But it's tough work. And we often fall short.

So this book is not about doing, it's about saying. Say this one simple prayer every day, and you will be happy forever. And it will even give you power to begin to live the Beatitudes.

So say this prayer, day by day. It will bring the power of heaven quietly into your life. That power will save you out of the worst jams you might be in right now. It will save you from all kinds of future jams too. Bit by bit, it will turn your life around.

So don't forget to say it today.

4. A Great Discovery

I KNEW a couple of struggling newly-weds. They were living in a tumble-down old house with woodlice in the rafters and water running through the ceiling. They were paying much more than they could afford for that tumble-down old house. Just struggling to survive. Then a little baby came to stay. And the struggle increased.

They prayed that God would make life easier.

At the time, there was a craze for something called 'The Jabez prayer' (1 Chr. 4:10). They tried that. But the strain remained. They tried saying other Bible verses every day. But still anxiety and stress ruled. This went on for four or five years.

Then, by some revelation, they made a Great Discovery. They began praying the Lord's Prayer every morning. Soon the strain and stress melted away. They became happier. Life became easier all round. Not overnight maybe, but pretty quickly.

Since that time, they have said this prayer every day. (That's not to say they don't forget sometimes. But they say it 99 percent of the time.) They say it as a family in the morning. They say it in the evening too. Sometimes they say it at midday or before an exam. And they are still blessed.

But maybe you say, "Why would this prayer bring such special blessings?"

The answer is very simple: Jesus told us to say it.

He said: *Therefore pray thus: Our Father in heaven* (Matt. 6.9). It's very clear. Nothing could be clearer. Jesus wants us to say exactly these words.

He didn't tell us to pray the 'Jabez prayer'. He didn't tell us to say the 'Four Spiritual Laws' or the Creed. He didn't even tell us to recite other Bible passages, like the Ten Commandments or the Beatitudes.

There's only one thing Jesus told us to say. He gave us this one little, short prayer. And he said, "Pray thus!"

He didn't say, "Pray something like this."

He didn't say "Here's a suggestion you might like to reflect on if ever you are in the mood for a bit of praying."

He didn't say, "Prayer is a good idea, and here's a general outline you can follow if you like."

No. He said, "Pray thus!" "Pray these words."

Some Bible translations don't make it quite clear. They say, "Pray like this." And I suppose people might take that to mean, "Pray (a bit) like this."

But that's not what Jesus's words mean. They are a clear instruction. "When you pray, pray exactly these words." "Pray thus."

So do it today.

5. Pray Thus

PRAY THUS, said Jesus.

Some folk don't like this idea. They think they needn't pray the exact words of the Our Father prayer. They feel it's more like something we can improvise on, like a twelve-bar blues. We can use it if we feel like it.

But Jesus said, "Pray thus!"

Some folk don't like being told how to pray.

They say, "Don't give me any set prayers. They're too mechanical. I want to pray from my heart, just like Jesus and his disciples did."

Let me tell you a secret. Set prayers were everywhere in the land of Israel in Jesus's time. The Israelites loved beautiful words. So set prayers were central to their lives.

They had set prayers for everything. Set prayers for their temple festivals and its many sacrifices. Set prayers for the New Moon, set prayers for the Sabbath. There were set words for the High Priest to bless the people. Set prayers for war. Set prayers for waking and resting. Set prayers for eating and drinking. Set prayers when you smelled fragrant spices, or saw the sea, or the flowers of spring, or a strange animal, or a rainbow, or a beautiful tree.

Most important of all, there was a prayer called the *Amidah,* the "Standing" prayer. The *Amidah* went back a long way. It was written long before Jesus was born.

The *Amidah* was central to the faith of ancient Israel. Every faithful Israelite stood and chanted the *Amidah* three times a day. And, each time, it took five or six minutes to chant.

Of course, people still had their own prayers. "Lord, bless my family, my home. Bless my wife, Susannah. Bless my son, Joseph. Bless my daughter, Hannah. Bless my father, my mother, my brother, my neighbour. Bless my flocks and my herds."

That was fine. First they said the *Amidah,* then they added their own prayers.

So when Jesus said, "Pray thus!" he meant "Pray this prayer. Forget the *Amidah.* I'm giving you a new prayer. Say it every day."

In fact, we know the apostles taught the early Christians to do just this. They prayed the Lord's Prayer three times a day, instead of the *Amidah.*[5]

So it's totally clear. Jesus gave us a set prayer. And he wants us to say it every day.

Of course, the Our Father is much shorter than the *Amidah.* It's a prayer for working people.

Jesus told us to pray this prayer. That means that when we say this little prayer we obey Jesus.

Obeying Jesus is always a good thing to do. It always brings great blessings.

Tetiana is a Ukrainian lady who was living in Bucha, near Kyiv, when the town was invaded in February 2022.[6] She had never been religious. But she knew the Our Father. So when the soldiers came, she said the Our Father every time she felt afraid. It enabled her to cope with the events around her.

The soldiers came to her house. They killed her dog. Then they turned their attention on her four-year-old granddaughter who told them to go back where they came from. In terror, Tetiana prayed the Our Father and the soldiers left, leaving the little girl alone. Between 400 and 500 civilians were tortured and killed in Bucha. But Tetiana prayed the Our Father and she and her family were saved.

She is convinced that this prayer alone got them through these terrible events. It changed her life. Now she believes in God and does what she can to help the people of her town through her local church. Her son is fighting. She is still praying.

So my best advice to you, or to anyone in trouble, or lost, or in debt, or perplexed, or hurt, or rejected, or addicted, or homeless, or hungry, or facing family breakdown or bad news, or worried about the future, or sick, or hopeless, or seeking the way, is this: "Pray the Our Father every day."

It will be to you a light in darkness, a guide in perplexity, a fountain of blessing poured out upon your head and upon all around you. The Son of

God told us to say these words. They contain the pure power of God who formed the heavens and the earth.

Don't believe me? Try it! Every day. Don't forget. Persist. And you will be blessed.

Say it with your family. If they will not join you, cry it aloud over their heads. Some bit of blessing will fall upon them.

Maybe you've been baptized but you have fallen away from faith and don't know the way back. Begin with this prayer. It will guide your feet home.

Maybe you never believed. Maybe your family never believed. But now you wonder if they were wrong. Yet the challenge of becoming a believer seems too great. You're afraid. Or you don't know where to start.

So start with this prayer. It will protect your soul and guide you forward step by step on the road of discipleship.

Some people, giants of faith, pray for hours a day. If one has the faith (and the time), that may be good. But this little prayer, the Our Father, is good for anyone, anytime. It's for busy people. It's where we all begin. And it's enough in itself.

Say it today and you're covered. Say it two or three times a day, and you're even more covered. It will align you with the plan of God. It will make Jesus's words your words. It will protect you. And it will open the door to endless blessings.

6. Great Shape

THE *OUR FATHER* prayer has a certain shape. It's pretty simple. Like a pastrami-on-rye sandwich with seven layers inside.

The top layer – the rye-bread – is a salutation to God, so we remember just who we're talking to. Since we are speaking, we use the word 'our'.

Our Father in heaven

We are talking to the great Creator of the universe. But he is also a Father to those who love him.

Then come the seven layers of the sandwich. These are seven requests or petitions. The first three are for the Father's sake. They concern his honour and his will. So they all feature the word 'thy' (your).

---

1. *Hallowed be thy name*

2. *Thy kingdom come*

3. *Thy will be done on earth as in heaven*

Then there are four layers, four petitions, for our own sake, to ask about our own needs. They all have the words 'our' or 'us'.

---

4. *Give us this day our daily bread*

5. *Forgive us our debts as we forgive our debtors*

6. *And lead us not into temptation*

7. *But deliver us from evil.*

Then to finish – like the bottom slice of rye-bread – there is a doxology. (A doxology is a set of words to glorify and praise God. Every good Jewish prayer ends with a doxology.) So it's back to 'thine'.

For thine is the kingdom, the power,
and the glory, now and for ever.
Amen.

Like I said, the seven layers in the middle are seven petitions. In the Bible, seven is always a special number. It's the number of perfection. Jesus made his prayer this way to show us that he has given us a perfect prayer. It's a prayer that says totally everything we need to say all the time. It covers all our needs.

All you and I need to do is say it.

OUR FATHER IN HEAVEN

7. There Is A Father

OUR FATHER. In Jesus's Aramaic language, it's a small word: *abun*. But it says a lot. You see, fathers are very important people. Like it or not, they have a big influence on who we become. But we don't get to choose our fathers.

Some fathers are great. Really good. As good as a man can be. Maybe he loves you, his child, with all his heart. He gives you good advice and wise guidance. He'd do anything for you.

Other fathers are less great.

Maybe you had an absent father. He left your mother before you were born. You never see him.

Other fathers are regular visitors. They come and visit your mother when they want money.

Other fathers have a good heart, but they seem to love the bottle more than their family.

Other fathers are angry and violent. They take out their frustration on their family in outbursts of rage.

Others are skirt-chasers. They spend their time and money on fancy women, breaking your mother's heart.

Others work non-stop. They see their kids just as a nuisance. Like Mr Banks in *Mary Poppins*, they got to "grind, grind, grind at that grindstone". They work day and night for career success. They think that will bring them the respect they crave and make them happy.

Some fathers combine several of these sad flaws. And some do even worse things than these.

But no matter what your father is like, good or bad, he can't make everything work out for you all the time. Sadly, he is not all-powerful. And then one day he won't be there anymore. And you'll be fatherless.

But can you imagine a father who is all good? He has no addictions, no wild rage, no vicious streak. He loves you with all his heart and always has time for you. He'll dry your tears if people hurt you.

What's more, he is totally all-powerful and all-wise to guide you, always. And he never dies. So he is always there to love you, help you, support you, guide you, and uphold you. Best of all, he has power. Real power. In fact, he has power enough to make you happy for ever.

The good news is that there is a such a Father.

He is the King of the Universe. He is the eternal Father in heaven. You can't see him. But he is there. He exists. He is really real. He truly loves you. He'll never let you down. He is reaching out to you. And you can find him and know him.

You only need to pray, "Our Father..."

8. You Are His Child

B UT MAYBE you reply, "Well, OK. Maybe there is a Father. But why would he care about me? I'm no-one special."

And that's a fair point. After all, the King of the Universe has plenty of other things to bother about apart from you, right?

I mean, you could run after some president or king or multi-billionaire and say to him, "Please, please, please, be my father and love me for ever and ever!" But he won't say "Yes." He'll set his bodyguards on you. He's got enough hangers-on.

So, if some earthly president or billionaire doesn't want you, then why would the King of the Universe want you? Why would he agree to be your Father?

The answer is that the Father wants you because he made you.

You didn't come into this world by accident.

You came into this world because the Father said, "I want Hazel, or Vanessa, or Joan, or Jim, or Karim, or Ravi or Mùchén or _ _ _ _ _ _ _ _ _ _ _ _ (write your own name here) to exist and to be my child." He made you. And he longs for his own little one that he made to turn to him and find him.

Unlike a president or a billionaire, he won't turn you away. Whoever comes to him, he welcomes. Whoever comes to him, he never turns away.

But, you may say, "If the Father loves me so much, why doesn't he tell me that?"

The reason he can't tell you is because you are not listening. You don't hear him. It's not because the Father doesn't have time for you. It's because you don't have time for him.

He waits for us to turn from continually trying to please other people. He waits for us to turn from our endless round of movies and social media and entertainment.

He is not short of time to listen to you. He has all the time in the universe. He longs for you to stop and to turn to him and say, "Father!" And then he will turn to you and say, "My child."

If you call him "Father", he will listen. Don't worry if you don't hear his voice speaking. Just call him, "Father", and you'll know that he is listening.

Once the Father is *your* Father, you are no longer lost. You are no longer an orphan. He will protect you. He will provide for your needs. He will bless your life. He promises you a hope and a future. He promises you happiness for ever.

So don't forget to call on him today, saying, "Our Father..."

9. All The Father's Children

THERE IS a Father. But he's not just *your* Father and he's not just *my* Father. He is *Our* Father, for he has many children.

And, like it or not, we belong to one another. We don't live alone. We live and pray together. And when we say "*Our* Father", we begin to make some important discoveries.

First, we realize that we are not Number One. The Father is Number One. Now that's a very important thing to realize. (Some people really do think they are Number One!) Nothing cures our egotism and vanity and mental illness quicker than realizing that we are not the centre of the universe.

No-one else is Number One either. Not your boss. Not your spouse or partner or ex-partner. Not your child. Not the people you admire or the people you dislike. No. The Father alone is Number One.

When we realize this, we lose the burden of our ego. We lose the burden of always looking out for number one. The Real Number One doesn't need you to look out for him. He will look out for you.

So the Father is Number One. But when we say "*Our* Father", we also come to see that the Father has many children.

It is no longer just me and the Father. Now I am part of a family. And the members of that family are all the people in the world who love the Father. When you say from your heart, "Our Father", you become part of the family of God. And so do I.

Within this family, Jesus is the great Son of God. Yet he calls us his brothers and sisters. He says, *Whoever does the will of my Father in heaven is my brother and sister and mother.* (Matthew 12:50) So when you call God "Father", you become part of this great family, where Jesus is the big brother.

This family has members all over the world, from Svalbard to Santiago, from Shanghai to San Francisco. It has members through all time, from Father Abraham and the prophets, through the disciples of Jesus, through all the ages, down to our own day.

This family also has members in your own town and maybe among your own relatives too. You are no longer alone. You have millions of brothers and sisters who pray to the Father. You need to begin to get to know them.

Also, when we say "Our Father", we realize that the Father loves his other children too. Yes, he loves you dearly. But he also loves all his children. And he wants us to treat one another fairly and kindly.

10. Who Art In Heaven

J ESUS tells us to say, *Our Father in heaven.* But, in his original Aramaic words, he actually said, "Our Father in the *heavens.*" So what did he mean by "the heavens"?

The people of Jesus's time didn't know as much about the cosmos as we do. But they looked up into the sky. There they saw the sun, moon, and stars, above the earth. Even in the old days, some of them knew that the earth was a ball or a sphere (Job 26:7; Isaiah 40:22). And on the earth below the heavens lived mankind and all earthly creatures.

Nowadays, we say the sun, moon, and stars are in "space", that is, in our solar system, our galaxy, or in the wide universe. Meanwhile, we think of "heaven" maybe as another dimension that we can't see. But for the people Jesus spoke to, it was all the same. "The heavens" were the place where the stars are. And the Father is in the heavens.

But, apart from that, the people Jesus spoke to were just like us. They knew that if you look into the sky, you don't see God. He may be *in* the heavens, but he's not visible. He's an invisible God.

And the Israelites knew well that their God was not just part of the heavens. He was the Creator of the heavens – of the sun, moon, and stars. He is over and above and beyond the heavens. Even the highest heavens cannot contain him. Yet, still, his presence is in the heavens. He made them to be his royal palace. And so, for them, it was fair to say that God dwells in the heavens. And that still makes sense even for us today.

Nowadays, we know more about the heavens than the people Jesus spoke to. (I imagine Jesus also knew a lot more about the heavens than he said.)

We know there are countless suns and planets and moons stretching so far we can't even imagine. Our great sun is only one star out of 100 billion in our galaxy. As for how many galaxies there are, no one knows. Estimates very from 100 billion up to trillions. NASA say the number of stars in the universe is maybe a sextillion or a septillion.

Travelling at the speed of light, it would take us 100,000 years to cross just our own local galaxy. As for the universe, the bit we can see is almost 100 billion light years across. But there's maybe much more.

Maybe there are even many universes – a multiverse – all inside one another. The mind staggers to consider these things. Yet what Jesus taught is still totally true. The heavens belong to the Father. He made them. And he dwells in them.

So that's why we say to him, *Our Father in heaven...*

11. The Father, The Maker

ONE OF the amazing things we learned last century is that the universe had a beginning. The first person to realize this was a Belgian physicist, Georges Lemaître.

In 1926, an American astronomer, Edwin Hubble, had shown that the "red shift" of light from distant stars meant that they were rapidly moving apart. The universe is expanding.

The next year, Lemaître proved that, since the stars were moving further apart, there had to be a time when it all began in one place.

He explained it to Einstein. But back then Einstein believed in a static universe which had always existed. So he initially rejected the idea. But he thought it over. Then, later, in 1933, he attended a lecture by Lemaître. Afterwards, he told him, "That is the most beautiful and satisfactory explanation of creation which I have ever heard."

That is how the physicists of the 1920s and 30s discovered that everything that exists began in a tremendous flash of light and power. (We now know this took place about 13.7 billion years ago, and we call it the Big Bang.) This made Einstein a believer in the existence of God.

Yet some people still say there is no God. They say the heavens just began all on their own.

But does that makes sense? Does anything just begin to exist all on its own? Think about it. Does anything create itself? Not even a slug or a snail or a bug creates itself. How could this whole complex universe begin to exist of its own accord? How could our wonderful little planet – so beautiful, so unique, so perfectly adapted for life, spinning like a sapphire in the middle of the infinite vastness of the cosmos – just begin to exist of its own accord?

Recently, I heard an interview with someone who is pioneering modern space travel. He said, "I used to say I was an atheist. But now I'm not so sure. Everything we are doing in space… I look up into the universe – and I say to myself, 'Where did it all come from? Who made all this?'"

It's impossible that the universe created itself. Nothing comes from nothing. Things don't create themselves. Someone made it all.

So there is no need to doubt that the Father exists. He made everything, by his power and wisdom, for his own good purpose and pleasure, billions of years ago. Then billions of years later, he made animals and mankind to live in his universe.

He did this so that we could look at his works and be amazed, and say "The heavens are telling the glory of God."

sad that he accepts
the deep time
myth — it undermining
his case

12. The Father Almighty

THE FATHER made the heavens out of nothing. He has preserved them for billions of years. He is still in control, still guiding, still active, still making new things in his cosmos every day. And from this, we learn four important things about our Father.

First, he is All-Powerful. He is God Almighty. His power is beyond anything we can ever think or imagine. All things are in his hand. He can do anything. He created the cosmos with a word. Nothing is impossible for God.[7] If he wants, he can divide the sea. If it pleases him, he can move mountains and dry up rivers. He sends fire and earthquake, drought and storm. He sends calm and shadow, rain and sunshine. He writes history. He can change the future. And, since nothing is impossible for him, I suppose he can even change the past.

Since he is All-Powerful, there is nothing he cannot do for you. His power for you is unlimited. He doesn't usually show his power in flashy ways. He hides himself. But he can bless you. He can turn your life around. He can make you happy for ever.

Second, the Father is All-Knowing. Physicists tell us that the physics at the Big Bang were complex beyond all imagining. It wasn't just an explosion. For a micro-second, the cosmos teetered on a knife-edge between existence and non-existence.

But the Father, by his knowledge and wisdom, made it into the lovely world of green fields and forests and blue skies that we live in today. Then he formed human beings from the dust of the stars. He made us to show his own great wisdom in us. And so he made us to be great artists, great athletes, great builders, great carers, great leaders, great medics, great nurses, great scientists, great orators, great thinkers. All our knowledge and skill and wisdom comes from him. He knows the past. He knows the future. He knows what might be. He knows everything that everyone has ever thought, or said, or done, throughout all of history. He knows the hidden secrets of every heart.

Since he is All-Knowing, he knows everything about you. There is nothing about you that is too hard for him to understand. The child has no problem that the Father cannot fix. He knows where you're coming from. He knows where you're going to. He can guide you all the way.

Third, the Father is All-Present. He is every-where. He made the cosmos and he inhabits it. But he exists beyond it. All he has made is like a speck of dust before him. He has infinite space to create as much as he wants for ever and ever and ever. Yet he is around us and within us. His Spirit and his power hold together the atoms of our world day by day. Every breath you draw, every beat of your heart, comes from him.

Since he is All-Present, he is with you every-where. If you are in trouble on a mountain-top, he can save you there. If you are in trouble on the sea, he is there. If you call to him in the desert, or in the country, or in the city, or under the ground, or on the moon, he is there. Wherever you speak to him, he hears you.

Fourth, the Father is Eternal. That doesn't just mean that he lives for all time. Yes, he inhabits time, but he is also beyond time. He lives for ever, but he also lives beyond forever. He always was. He always is. He always will be.

Since he is Eternal, he was there before you existed. He wished you into existence on the day you were conceived. He protected you in your mother's womb. He will be with you every day of your mortal life, in all you do. He will be with you in death. He will be with you after your spirit leaves your body.

This is your Father in the heavens, Almighty, All-Wise, All-Present, Eternal. Mighty to bless you, wise to instruct you, present to help you, in all time and for ever.

I once heard a comment by a person who didn't believe in God. For him, life was a comfortless, sad, pitiless, lonely business, ending in pain and death.

He said, "What a difference it would make, if only we knew that the universe loves us."

But we know better than that. The best news of all is that the King of the universe loves us. Beneath our daily struggles and strains, beneath our joys and sorrows, beneath our working, sleeping, and eating, beneath our little lives and our impending deaths, lie the everlasting arms of the Father.

He loves us. He is always there to catch us. He commands his universe to look after us in all our ways. And why would we not love him too?

THREE PETITIONS

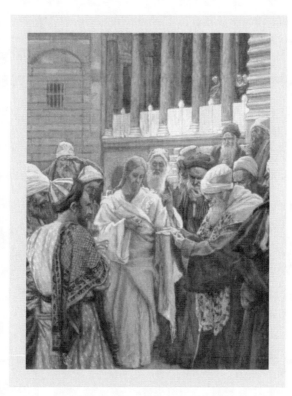

FOR THE
FATHER'S SAKE

13. The First Petition

WE CAN SEE, as we go along, that Jesus has got all the words of his prayer in the right order.

You see, to become children of God, the first thing we must do is call him Father. But the second thing we must do is thank him. That's what we do in this first petition.

These four words in English – *Hallowed be your Name* – are just two words in Jesus's Aramaic prayer. But like the opening words (Our Father), they say a tremendous amount.

When we say "Hallowed be your name", we begin to praise God. This is totally life-changing. I know of a man who didn't believe in God. But one day he was feeling grateful for his life and for all the good things he had. He wanted to thank someone, but he didn't know who to thank. So he went to bed and spoke into the air and said, "Thank you." Then he fell asleep. When he woke the next morning, the world was changed. Everything was beautiful. And he realized that overnight he had come to believe in God.

Thanking or praising God can totally change us. It puts us in a position where we say to the Father,

"Everything I have comes from you. I am grateful for your goodness to me." And, when we say that, it opens up doors and pathways from heaven for God to bless us.

There's not just one way to thank God. We can look to the sky and say, "Thank you." Or we can say, "I praise you for all your goodness to me." Or we can say, "Bless the Lord, O my soul." Or, like Jesus says here, we can say, "Hallowed be your name."

Hallowed is not an everyday word. But it comes from the word "holy". "Holy" is a little word that says a lot. It means special, honoured, set apart, and filled with glory and power. So when we say "Hallowed be your name", we are praying that God's name will be honoured and blessed as it deserves to be, for he is special and glorious. It's like saying, "I thank you and praise you because you are amazing, and I pray that all the world will honour you." But we can say it in just a few words.

And that's a good thing to say. Call God's name holy every day and your life will be transformed. Those who bless him, he blesses. Those who honour him, he honours. His own power and blessing and glory and holiness will flow down into your own life.

14. The Hallowed Name

BUT WHAT did Jesus mean when he said, "Hallowed be your Name"? Is *your Name* just a way of saying "your reputation"? (Like when we talk about someone's "good name".) Or is there more to it than that?

I think there is more to it than that. And to understand we need to talk about names and titles.

A person can have a name and a title. Let's imagine someone with a big job. His title might be President or Chancellor or Chief Executive Officer. But his title is not his name. His name is perhaps Bob Smith. His interns may call him by his title, "Mr President". His wife and mother call him by his name, "Bob". Business acquaintances may call him "Bob" or "Mr Smith". His kids call him "Dad", which is a title, but a special title reserved for his children.

In the same way, God Almighty has titles and names. His titles include God, Lord, King of Kings, Ancient of Days, El Shaddai (Almighty God), El Elyon (God Most High), HaQadosh (the Holy One), and, for his children, Father. But these are all titles, not names.

But God has names as well. In fact, he has two

real personal names which he has revealed to us.[8] These are Jehovah and Jesus. And they are closely related.

Jehovah is God's name revealed in the Old Testament. Although it is usually spelt "Jehovah", it should really be pronounced "Y'ho**vah**", with the accent on the last syllable.[9] This is by far the most common name all through the Old Testament. It appears there almost 7,000 times. (He is definitely Number One there.) But usually you can't see it in our translations. This is because the translators write it as "LORD" (with small capitals). The reasons why they do this lie deep in the history of Bible translation. But it might be better if they wrote "Jehovah" or "Yehovah".

Jehovah means, "I will be-I am-I was." And Jehovah said that whenever his people prayed to him with that name, he would help them and bless them. *In every place where I cause my Name to be called upon, I will come to you and bless you* (Exodus 20:24).

But Christians accept Jesus's teaching that God is Trinity (Matt. 28:19). So we may well ask, "Who is Jehovah? Is he the Father, or the Son, or the Spirit?" The answer is that it's not always clear. Sometimes the name Jehovah means the Father. Other times it means the Son, when he appears as a man, as he did to Abraham, Jacob, and others. The Trinity is a mystery not fully explained in the Old Testament. So Jehovah can be the Father and the Son.

The second name, "Jesus", is the name of the Son when he was born in Bethlehem. In Hebrew and Aramaic it is pronounced **Yeshua** – the accent on the middle syllable.[10] It means "Jehovah saves." So, like I said, it's linked to his Old Testament name, Jehovah. But it carries with it a promise – Jehovah will save. For that reason, it has greater power than any other name.

Now back to our first question. What did Jesus mean when he said, "Hallowed be your name"? He didn't say "Hallowed be your title." He wasn't talking about any of God's titles. He must have meant one of God's names. And since Jesus was the Son speaking about the Father, he must have meant the name Jehovah.

By the time of Jesus, the leaders of Jerusalem and Judah had banned speaking the name Jehovah for everyone. The only exception was that the High Priest had to speak the Name once a year on the Day of Atonement.

Their idea was to stop people breaking the third commandment: *You shall not take the Name of Jehovah your God in vain.* But it was a bad idea. In banning the Name, they went way too far. For God never told them to forbid speaking his Name. Remember, he offered salvation to his people in this Name of Jehovah. Yet the leaders of Israel prohibited the people from saying it.

But Jesus would not have agreed with banning

the Holy Name. So instead he went back to what the commandment said: People should honour or "hallow" the Name of Jehovah. That means, I think, that Jesus really did speak the Name of Jehovah. I imagine he encouraged his disciples to speak it too. And we can imagine that the leaders of Judah did not like this one little bit.

Some folk nowadays don't like this idea either. They don't think Jesus went around speaking the Name which the Judean hierarchy had forbidden. Maybe they think he wouldn't have defied the authorities like this. Or maybe they just can't accept that anyone may ever speak the Name.

But Jesus was never much impressed by the Judean leaders or their rules. And as for the Name being forbidden, like I said, Jehovah told his people to pray in his name. He never banned it. So Jesus told his people to return to the true sense of the third commandment: to honour the Name of Jehovah. That means saying it at the right time, in the right way.

So it is perfectly OK for you and me to speak the name of Jehovah. But now we have an even greater Name. A name above all names. The name of Jesus – Jehovah saves. This is the name of power that Christians have been given. It is greater than all names, because it carries within it the promise of Jehovah's salvation.

We should hallow both names.

15. The Second Petition

NEXT, Jesus tells us to say, *Thy Kingdom come*. Let me start with a story.

I live in Belgium, between France and Holland. People here speak French and Dutch. Yet Belgium isn't like its neighbours, especially France. There are many differences. But the biggest ones are in the area of faith and religion.

The French cut off the heads of their kings and clerics in their Revolution. Since then, they have been ardently anti-religious. Yes, there are religious people in France – Christians and now many Muslims. But all the institutions of the French state are *laïque*, that is, secular and functionally atheistic.

Belgium is different. Belgium has a Catholic king ruling a Catholic nation. The Church plays a big part in state rites. Public prayers are sung for the king twice a year. The best schools in the country are Jesuit schools. Most Belgians are baptized, and have attended these schools, and received much Christian teaching.

Some years back, my daughter was playing at the home of a friend, Marie. When I came to pick her up, her parents offered me tea and we sat down to chat. Her father told me he was a Buddhist.

That's why he preferred tea to coffee. He said the Church had never convinced him. Buddhism gave him peace. He believed in reincarnation. If we do good here, we will come back in another body with a better status. That gave him moral direction and hope for the future.

I listened to what he said. Then I said that I also had hope for the future because I was a Christian. I said that God will raise up the faithful in new bodies. Then we will live a new life here on earth, with Jesus the King Messiah ruling in Jerusalem.

His jaw didn't actually hit the floor. But it was clear, from his fixed gaze, that, in all his years of Christian education, he had never heard such a thing. But, frankly, that's not surprising. For, in many churches the standard teaching on this topic is that the faithful die, their souls go to heaven, and that's the end of the story. In theory, these folk all believe in the resurrection of the dead. They confess it in the Creed. But they don't talk about it. They can't see how resurrection fits in with this idea of the soul going to live for ever in heaven.

Yet this idea – the soul going to heaven and staying there – comes more from Greek philosophy than the Bible. The Bible teaches clearly that Jesus is coming back to earth to set up God's kingdom here in this world. This is the 'kingdom' that Jesus means when he tells us to say 'Thy kingdom come'.

16. Thy Kingdom Come

SO WHEN we pray for God's kingdom to come, we are praying for Jesus to come back and rule the earth.

God's kingdom isn't quite the same as Paradise. Paradise is where the spirits of the faithful go when they die. (It's the Land o' the Leal.) We can't pray for Paradise to come. Paradise already exists, although we can't see it.

Those who are now in Paradise (like my mother) are in the near presence of God, in a place of joy and peace. Yet Paradise is also a place of waiting. The folk there are waiting, just like us, for Jesus to return to this world – to smash into our time and space – and bring God's Kingdom into our world.

On that day, their dead bodies will be raised, even those who have been cremated or have rotted in the grave for 3,000 years, or have been eaten by beasts, or birds, or fish. The spirits of the faithful dead will return to renewed bodies. These new bodies will be perfect, beautiful, and deathless. This is the resurrection of the dead.

In the same way, the faithful who are alive when Jesus comes will be transformed. They too will receive new bodies. And they will live with the faithful of all the ages in the Messiah's kingdom.

So we have three stages to think about: this world, Paradise, and the Messiah's Kingdom in Jerusalem. But even that is just the beginning.

The Messiah's kingdom will endure for a while – for one thousand years – then God will renew everything on an even greater scale. There will be *a new heaven and a new earth* greater than anything before. There will be an even greater new Jerusalem which will descend from the heavens onto the earth. The children of God will inherit the heavens and the earth and be happy for ever.

But for the faithless, it will be different. When they die, they will be held in Hades, a place of detention, till the end of the Messiah's thousand-year kingdom. Then they will be judged. Some will find mercy, especially if they showed mercy to the Lord's people (Matt. 10:41–42). But others will not.

You can read about all this in the last chapters of the New Testament (Revelation 21–22).

But even all that is not the end. For the God of glory has new things planned, bit by bit, for ever. He is always doing new things.

But the first stage in his great plan is the coming of the kingdom. That's why we pray *Thy kingdom come*. When we say these words we are asking for all these things to happen. And we are asking that our own personal future, as children of the Father, will be within the Father's Kingdom.

17. *The Third Petition*

THESE WORDS, at first glance, seem to say the same thing as *Thy Kingdom come.* After all, when God's Kingdom comes, people will do his will on earth, just as the angels do in heaven. But these words actually say something more. They talk about HERE AND NOW.

You see, the coming Kingdom is in the future. It hasn't come yet. We have no control over when it will come. But doing God's will is something that can happen today. It is something *we* can do today. It is something that can happen in the lives of *people around you* today.

Let's start with you and me. We can do the will of the Father today. That will please him. BUT to do this, we need two things. We need to *know* his will. And we need the desire and the power to do it.

Knowing the will of God in every situation is not easy. But the simplest way to learn God's general will for us is to read the Bible. The Ten Commandments tells us most of it. We should honour God, worship him and not idols, love our parents and our families, not kill, not be unfaithful in marriage, not steal, not tell lies about people, not envy them. These are the basics. Do these and life will be happier for you and everyone around. And the Bible has heaps more advice on the best way to live.

But even when we do know the will of God, we need the desire and the power to do it. It can be hard to honour your parents. It can be tempting to be unfaithful in marriage, or to steal or lie. But when we pray *Thy will be done,* God gives us the heart and the strength to do his will.

Then there are times when you want to know the will of God, but the answer is not in the Bible? What should I study? Who should I marry? Where should I work and live? Which school should my kids go to? Which parties should I allow them or forbid? Which medical treatment should I choose? In these cases, keep praying *Thy will be done,* and ask for wisdom, and God will show you what is best.

When we say *Thy will be done* it gets us working for God's will to be done on earth. Over the years, these words have led people to build hospitals, schools, and churches, to translate Bibles, help the poor, work for justice – to build a better society. They can inspire us to do great things too.

But don't think you need to be the next Mother Teresa. There are people all around you needing a kind word, or a smile, or an encouragement. Do God's will on earth and change the world in your own small corner.

FOUR PETITIONS

FOR OUR SAKE

18. The Fourth Petition

WHEN WE say *Give us today day our daily bread*, we are asking for everything we need for life.

We are asking for food to eat and drink to drink. We are asking for clothes to wear and a roof over our heads. We are asking for useful work that will bring us enough to live on. We are asking to be healthy. We are asking for a spouse and a family so we don't have to live and die alone.

There's no need to spell out every detail. He understands. But, if you want, you can add your own special requests at the end of your prayer.

The Father wants us to live happily in his world. That doesn't mean he'll give us every luxury. We don't need that. But he wants us to have enough to be well and to help others, with a place to stay, with good health, with people to love and be loved and call our own, and with lives that go straight, and are not all broken. So he'll provide what we need.

There's a passage in the book of Proverbs says this nicely. It says, *In all your ways acknowledge him and he will make your paths straight* (Prov. 3:6).

But, when you're praying for your daily bread, there's a couple of things worth remembering.

connect?

First, God normally blesses us through our work. If you don't want to work, you may not be blessed. So find a job, or make a job, and get busy and do your best without complaining.

Second, the Bible teaches that God is generous to those who are generous and tight-fisted to those who are tight-fisted. *A generous soul will prosper, and whoever blesses others will be blessed* (Prov. 11:25). *He who sows sparingly will reap sparingly, and he who sows generously will reap generously* (2 Cor. 9:6).

So, if you want God to prosper you, you should learn to give. In Old Testament times, the Israelites gave a tenth, or tithe, of their income to God and to the poor. That's still a good guide.

But maybe you say, "I could never give a tenth of my salary! I can't even live on what I'm getting."

Fair enough. Learn God's faithfulness by starting small. This month, give one percent of your income. If it goes OK, raise it to two percent. If that goes OK, raise it some more. You'll find he is faithful and he will provide all you need.

You can give some of this money to your church. But you can give to other places too. I'm a great believer in the work of the Bible Societies, who subsidize the cost of Bibles so everyone can have one. The best thing you can ever do for another person is to give them the living word of God.

19. Prosperity Doctrine

THERE'S ONE more thing to add here. Some churches teach what is called "Prosperity Doctrine" or "Health and Wealth Gospel".

The Health and Wealth Gospel is all about what we can get right now. The people who preach this gospel say that, if you send them money, and if you have faith, God will make you rich.

Giving money to God is a good thing. But true Christian "good news" isn't about getting rich. It's about God sending his Son to die for our sins, to bring us back to the Father, and give us eternal life.

So the Health and Wealth Gospel is half-true. It's half-true because God *does* want his children to be happy and healthy. But it's half-false when it says God always *has* to make us rich. And it's false when it says people lack money because they lack faith.

God *can* bless us with all we need. If we work hard, and are generous, and don't spend what we don't have, he often does. But he doesn't *have* to do anything. He owes us nothing. He is free to give or not to give. He is God.

In fact, in addition to there being blessings of plenty and prosperity, there are also blessings of trouble and adversity. Let me explain.

Jesus says, *Blessed are you when people insult you, persecute you and falsely say all kinds of evil against you because of me* (Matthew 5:11). That is to say, there are times when our faith leads us to clash with bad people, and they will target us.

All through the ages, God's servants have been robbed, mocked, and killed for their faith. So there can be a Gospel of Suffering and Poverty, the opposite of the Health and Wealth Gospel.

It was faith in God that put Jesus on the cross. If the Health and Wealth Gospel is true, then Jesus was a big loser with no faith.

But, in the end, the real winners are those who endure for God. Look what else Jesus says. To those who are persecuted for his sake he says, *Rejoice and be glad, because great is your reward in heaven* (Matt. 5:11). In other words, God sees faithful suffering, and a greater blessing than earthly prosperity awaits these people in the time to come. The calling of adversity overrules the general rule of daily blessing. But it brings greater blessings in the end.

The Real Gospel is about living to inherit God's Kingdom. It's not about getting rich in our short, mortal lives here and now. To have too much money is destructive for people. So he may not give us all we want. But, if we pray *Give us this day our daily bread,* then he gives us all we need to serve him and walk quietly through his world.

20. The Fifth Petition

THE PREVIOUS section – *Our daily bread* – is about our physical needs. But this section – *Forgive us our debts* – is about our spiritual needs. The Lord knows we think more about our stomachs than our souls. That's why he deals with our bodily needs first. But he knows our souls are worth more than our bodies. So he deals with our spiritual needs next.

Being in debt isn't good. Borrow money you don't have and lenders control you. They charge interest. If you can't pay, you end up poor, in court, or in jail. So, to be happy, don't get into debt. Better eat grass than borrow money you can't repay.

In the same way, if we commit a crime, we must pay our debt to society. That's why law-breakers are fined and go to jail. But what we don't see is that we also owe amends to the Judge of all the earth, who knows all we have ever done. So we must beg him to cancel our debt.

Other Bibles say *Forgive us our sins* or *Forgive us our trespasses*. But it all adds up to the same thing. It means we've gone where we shouldn't have gone. We've done what we shouldn't have done. We've offended the Father and other people. We've spoilt our character and brought guilt on our soul.

But when we say *Forgive us our debts,* we admit that we have done wrong. We are not covering it up any more. We are saying plainly, "I have done what I should not have done. I'm guilty."

Now this is bad news and good news.

It's bad news, obviously, because we have done wrong and offended the Father.

But it's good news because we have admitted it. When we admit it, we open the door to healing.

Let's imagine you are feeling unwell. You go to the doctor and he says, "I'm sorry, my friend. You have bilharzia." There are two ways you can reply.

You can say, "I don't have bilharzia. I've been healthy all my life. Stupid quack! What do you know about bilharzia anyway?" And you can walk out the door. In that case, the parasites will kill you.

Or you can say, "What can I do, doc?" Then the doctor may reply, "Well, we have a treatment for this. If you follow my advice, you can be totally healed."

Our debts and trespasses are like parasites in our souls. Doctor Jesus says they'll kill us. But the good news is that he can forgive our offenses, and pardon our guilt, and heal us. Doctor Jesus has the power to do this, to heal our souls and our spirits.

Now this is important. You see, just like we need to accept the doctor's diagnosis to be healed, so we need to accept Jesus's diagnosis to be saved. He says we should admit our sins, saying, *Forgive us our debts*. If we do that, he'll heal us. But if we don't admit our sins, then, like the person who says, "I don't have bilharzia", we'll perish.

This is a basic truth of the Christian faith. It's only when we realize that we are sinners that we can be saved.

Two robbers hung on crosses beside Jesus (Luke 23:39–43). They were lawless men. They had stolen. They were violent. They had probably spilled innocent blood. They did it casually, not caring. Then they ended up hanging on crosses.

One robber blamed everyone else for his fate. You can see him blaming his father, his mother, the system, the government, God. He yells at Jesus, "Aren't you the Messiah? Save yourself and us!" Although his own words admit that Jesus is the Messiah, he blames Jesus because he is still on the cross. "Why have you not saved me, Mr Messiah?"

But the other robber is different. He says, "We're getting what our sins deserve." He knows he's done wrong. Sure, others had a bad influence on him. But he sees that ultimately he's the one responsible for his own choices and his own deeds. And that's why he's on the cross.

After saying this, he says that Jesus is not guilty. "This man has done nothing wrong." He too sees that Jesus is the Messiah. In fact, he sees that Jesus, even Jesus hanging on a cross, can save him. So he asks Jesus to remember him. And Jesus gives this one rough sinner a free ticket to the Land o' the Leal. *Amen, I tell you, Today you will be with me in Paradise* (Luke 23:43).

But it was when he confessed his own faults that he saw that Jesus could save him. All this took place right there on the cross, as Jesus shed his blood to buy a pardon for all who confess their sins.

The only obstacle between us and the Father is our debts and trespasses. We have thought only of ourselves and done wrong to others. But when we admit our sins, the obstacle is removed. It's one of the best things we can ever do. Just stop blaming other people – parents, husband, wife, boss. And say, "It's my fault. I've done wrong. I'm to blame." Yes, of course other people influenced us. But the final blame for our faults is ours alone. Admitting this is a vital step to spiritual health and happiness.

One more thing. The more we read the Bible, the more we see we are sinners. Folk who don't read the Bible find it easy to say, "I've done nothing wrong." But really they just have very low standards. But people who read the Bible learn God's high standards of right and wrong. The better they know these standards, the more they know they have fallen short.

That's why we all need to say every day, *Forgive us our debts.*

21. As We Forgive Our Debtors

B UT THERE'S one more thing. *Forgive us our debts* is the only petition that comes with a rider or a condition – *as we forgive our debtors.* We must forgive other people and not harbour anger or bitterness against them. We are not their judges. God is.

Jesus makes it clear that this is important. He adds, at the end of the prayer, *If you forgive people their trespasses, then your heavenly Father will forgive you. But if you do not forgive people their trespasses, neither will the Father forgive you* (Matt. 6:14–15).

Now let's be very honest here. Forgiving others isn't easy. It can be really difficult. After all, there are hundreds of ways in which people can do you serious wrong.

There's your trust. They can lie to you and cheat you. They can make promises, then just break them. There's your reputation. They can slander and insult you, so that everyone thinks ill of you. There's your property. They can cheat you out of money or steal or damage your possessions. There's your body. They can abuse, attack, hurt, wound, or cripple you. There's your family. They can attack, mistreat, or even kill the people you love most.

They can do all these things, and not show the slightest sign of regret. They walk off laughing, wiping their mouth, patting their wallet.

And yet there is something deeper that hurts even more. The way they treat you shows they don't give a damn about you. Their attitude says that you are worth nothing at all. They feel they have the right to treat you any way they like.

So forgiving is not easy. Yet the Lord tells us we must forgive. And there are good reasons why.

To start with, although other people have hurt us, we have also hurt other people. We maybe say, "I didn't do anything as bad as he did to me." But, still, we've all done wrong. We've treated other people like they weren't worth much. We've bad-mouthed them, or mocked them, or trashed them, so they felt they weren't worth much. And maybe we've done worse things than that.

So, since we've done wrong, it's only fair that we deal gently with others who do us wrong. If we can't do that, it shows we are not sorry for what we have done. But if we do forgive, then it shows that we really do see our own faults.

Of course, if we can't see our own faults, then the Lord can't forgive us. It's linked to our request that the Father forgive *our* sins. The way we forgive others is a measuring rod of just how far we have admitted and renounced our own sins.

Yet still it's not easy. But maybe we can find

some steps to help us on the way.

First, we must accept that forgiving bigger sins takes time. If a bloke in a shop cheats you out of five euros, you don't lose any sleep over it. You say, "OK. I'll survive. God forgive him." But if someone you know really well, someone you totally trusted, cheats you out of many thousands of euros, then forgiving is a much bigger process.

You can make the person aware of what they have done. You can go to them, explain it as you see it, and say, "I feel you have done me wrong." This is what Jesus told us to do (Matt. 18:15–17). Maybe the other person will listen to you and say, "Yes, you're right. I did wrong. How can I make it right?" Then you discuss it, and make peace.

But often, of course, they are not sorry at all. And sometimes you just need to let it go at that.

But Jesus also outlines another step. If you and the person who did you wrong are both in the one church, then take the matter to the church leaders. Maybe they will help and mediate. In that case, maybe you can make peace, and maybe the other person will be stopped from hurting others. But, on the other hand, maybe the church leaders cannot or will not deal with it. And, in that case, once again, you need to let it go.

So now you are in the position where someone has committed a crime against you, but they just don't care. And no-one else cares. You'll have to deal with a lot of anger and desire for revenge. You may wake, night after night, really wanting to harm them. This is a normal response to how they treated you. But the vital first step to forgiveness is to say, "I won't take revenge."

Next, you must tell yourself, "I am on the road to forgiving this hurt. I know it will take time. It might take years. But, in the end, I will let it go."

The anger will keep coming back, day after day. But *cease from anger and turn from wrath* (Ps. 37:8). Day after day, continue to pray, *Forgive us our sins, as we forgive those who sin against us.* You can also say, "Lord, forgive this person for what he or she did. I don't know how to forgive. Please help me."

Also, it's very tempting to tell others about the injustice. But that just prolongs the bitterness. So try not to do it.

This may take months, even years. The mental anguish you will suffer is one more sin on this person's account. But you must forgive that too.

It may take five or ten or twenty years till the bitterness goes. And you won't be in a hurry to trust that person again. But in the end, you will be able to look the situation in the face and say, "By the grace of God, I am not bitter. By the grace of God, I have forgiven, as God forgives me." And the Lord, the just judge, will do justice in the end.

22. The Sixth Petition

DIFFERENT Bibles translate these words in different ways. Some say *Lead us not into temptation* or *Do not bring us to temptation.* Others say *Do not bring us to testing* or *Do not bring us to the time of trial.* All these translations are right, because the original Aramaic and Greek words can mean *testing* or *temptation* or *trial.*

You see, any time we are *tempted*, we're also *tried* and *tested*. For instance, the Apostle Paul reminds the Galatians of *your testing by my bodily condition* (Gal. 4.14). What he means is: I arrived at your door sick; that was a burden for you; it *tested* or *tried* your love for me; it *tempted* you to ignore me.

When we are *tempted* to do wrong, our strength of character is *tested*. In the same way, when we are *tested*, we are *tempted* to do wrong. (Like when folk go into exams with answers up their sleeves.) So *testing, tempting,* and *trial* are much the same.

Jesus wants his words to cover all this range of situations. They can mean "Don't let me be led into temptation to sin." Like when someone offers you a bribe to make you cheat, or lie, or turn a blind eye, or any one of 10,000 other temptations to do wrong. We ask that such things won't come our way.

But Jesus's words can also mean, "Don't let me brought to trial." Christians are sometimes dragged into court for trial. Maybe someone accuses them to the local authorities. They must answer serious charges about not honouring local gods or customs. We are asking to be spared from this too.

But there is yet another sense to Jesus's words. One time, he was speaking about dreadful trials that will come upon the world in the future. And he said, *Pray that you may be able to escape all that is about to happen, and that you may be able to stand before the Son of Man* (Luke 21:36). So we are praying to be saved from trials that will come upon the world and to stand guiltless before Jesus when he comes.

In the same way, Jesus is speaking of the judgement that will begin when he returns. One day, God will judge people according to their deeds (Rev. 20:12). That will be a fearful day. BUT those who love and follow Jesus will not face this judgement. Jesus is very clear about this. He says,

> *Whoever hears my word and believes him who sent me has eternal life and does not come into trial. He has passed from death into life* (John 5.24).

What Jesus means is that, when he comes back, all who believe in God and have tried to keep Jesus's teachings (*hear my word*) will not be judged, but will be raised to life and honour.

But those who have not believed in God, who have not kept Jesus's teachings, really will be judged according to what they've done. On that day, some may find mercy. But others won't.

So when we pray *Lead us not into temptation*, we are asking God to spare us in all these ways.

Yet there's only one problem with all this. It's this: Sometimes the Lord *does* test his people. The Bible says so. He tested Abraham (Gen. 22.1). He tested Job (Job 1:9–12). He tested the Israelites (Deut 8:2–3). He even tested Jesus (Matt. 4:1).

And, just to make things tougher still, the apostle James says God tempts no-one, but it's our own lawless passions that tempt us to sin. After all, why would God tempt us? Does he want us to sin?

The answer to this puzzle, I think, is that James means we can't blame God when we sin. It's not the Father's fault if we cave in to our weakness.

Yet it's true that God tests us. Just like he tested Abraham, Job, and Jesus, sometimes he tests us too.

Why does he do this? There are several reasons.

First, testing makes us stronger. Every time our body beats a disease, our immune system gets stronger. In the same way, each time we beat temptation, our spiritual strength increases.

Second, testing increases our faith. For instance, God may put us under such big financial pressure that we don't even know where our next meal is coming from. In such situations, we have to look to him alone and learn that he provides. In that way, we learn to trust him alone.

Third, testing makes us humble, but it leads to joy. Testing makes us feel threatened and weak and stressed and unable to cope. Facing exams is not easy. You pull out your hair and your eyebrows. You fear failure and disgrace. But when you pass your exams, you are filled with joy.

Imagine you want to be a nurse or a physio. But you don't study at all. You flunk every test and fail the whole course. You wouldn't feel so proud.

But if you pass, you can say, "I did it! I passed!" That's what it's like with God's tests. When we pass them, we have happiness, confidence, and joy. And the Lord is pleased with us.

Fourth, sometimes God wants to bless us, but he wants us to pass his test first. That was how it was with Abraham (Gen. 22:15–18). And sometimes that is how it is with us too. Before he will bless us, we must pass a test. He will not test us more than we can bear (1 Cor. 10:13). But we must pass the test.

Like Isaac Newton said, "Trials are medicines which our gracious and wise physician gives because we need them. Let us trust his skill and thank him for the prescription."

That's why James tells us to be joyful when we face trials and temptations, because the testing of our faith makes us perfect and complete (James 1:2–4). And that's how we all want to be, isn't it?

23. The Seventh Petition

HOW WOULD you like a shield around you, night and day, to keep you from all harm? Well, here it is. That's what these five words – *But deliver us from evil* – are all about. Make a list of all the things you fear most. Go on. Write it down. Whatever you like. For you or the folk you love. Here's some suggestions for starters:

- aeroplane crashes
- cancer
- car accidents
- death and damnation
- dementia and senility
- demonic delusion
- divorce
- famine
- homelessness

- insanity
- kidnapping
- loneliness
- mugging
- poverty
- slander
- shooting
- torture
- war

Look at all the things you fear. Then say, "Father, deliver us from evil." Name the things you fear most. "Deliver us from drowning," "Deliver us from robbery," and so on. And claim his protection.

Being protected from evil is a vital ingredient in the recipe of How to Be Happy. Yet some folk don't grasp what we are asking here. This word, 'evil', means everything bad. So what these words really mean is "Keep us safe from bad things." We're asking the Father to shield us from everything bad. This means, first, that God will protect us from the devil's power. Demonic powers can possess people and make them commit terrible crimes – shootings, knife attacks – and then kill themselves. Fearful things can happen when such powers enter a person's soul. God can protect you from this. But avoid anything linked with these dark powers: ouija boards, horoscopes, mediums, fortune-tellers. Steer clear of them. Tell him you're sorry if you've used them, and ask him to wash you clean.

But these words also protect you from other bad things. Do you think the Father only cares about your soul and not your body? He does care. He made them both. And, remember, he is Almighty. He can shield you from every evil. He can make evils fly over your head. You will look in wonder at the troubles that have missed you. This is true blessing: to be shielded and delivered from evil.

Maybe you wake in the middle of the night with awful nightmares. Perhaps you see someone stealing your child. Or you see yourself making some terrible error that will ruin you. You wake up shaking. Many such nightmares are threats sent by demons to ruin our sleep and make us live in fear.

But there is good news.

First, God allows such nightmares because he wants us to pray that they never happen. Every time the nightmare occurs, just say, "Father, deliver us from evil. May that never happen." Like an ad-blocker, it will be added to your list of protection.

But it's also good to pray for God's peace before you lie down. Say the *Our Father*. Then say, "Father, shield us this night with the blood of Jesus and let no evil dreams affright our rest." Then lie down and sleep in peace.

Years ago, when I passed my driving test, my father said to me, with real concern (for he knew what I was like), "You are now licensed to use a machine that can kill people – your passengers, and pedestrians and motorists and little children."

I never thought much about his words at the time. Yet God's grace protected me. And later, the weight of his words sank in. So, over the years, whenever I got in a car, I asked God to protect me, my passengers, and everyone on the road around me. And I'm really grateful that, in all my years of driving, I've never hurt anyone. Sure, there have been bashes and scrapes. Once I almost hit a woman who jumped out in front of me from behind a parked truck.) But no one has been hurt. This is blessing: to be protected from evil.

When I was 21, I'd a summer job with a landscape gardener in my home town in Scotland. It was a cowboy outfit. The bosses cheated the customers. They didn't do the work they were paid for. The workers stole from the boss.

So one time I was sent with two of these men to do the gardens in a new housing development. I was the driver. When we arrived there, I saw them eyeing up some building materials on the site. I could see they were planning to steal this stuff. So, at the end of the day, I came back to the van, and it was filled with stolen stuff.

I told them, "Take it out. I'm not driving away with it."

Amazingly, they did what I said. But, driving back, they were boiling. "What's it to you?" they said.

I said, "The Bible says you shall not steal."

They jeered at me and cursed me. "Just you wait," they said. "We're gonna put you in hospital!"

I was a bit concerned about this. That evening, I read Psalm 34, where the Lord says his angel will defend me from those who want to hurt me.

A week later, I was strangely alone at the depot late on a Friday afternoon. They screeched in on a truck with two friends. They were red-eyed drunk. Four-against-one, wielding planks, they came for me like a flood. "Into the tool shed, you!" (There were a lot of sharp tools in that tool shed.)

I ducked into the office, seconds ahead of them. I hoped the secretary might just be there. Instead, a man I'd never seen was standing at the counter – an ordinary-looking Scottish working bloke, about forty-five years old – standing doing nothing.

He smiled at me. I found that reassuring. I stood beside him.

I asked, "No one here?"

He smiled and nodded, as if to say, "As you see." So I stood with this silent man. Outside, these lawless men raged up and down, yelling at me to come out. I saw them looking through the big glass window. But it was as if they couldn't see me. And they didn't come in.

I told my silent companion, "They're after me." He smiled again and nodded. I could see he knew they were after me. But he didn't ask why.

I stood there for some twenty minutes. The man stood quietly, in no hurry, as if waiting for no-one.

I said, "Will I go out and see what they want?" He smiled and shook his head, as if to say, "I wouldn't do that." So I stayed with him. Finally, my enemies drove away. After five minutes, I said, "I think I can go now." He smiled. I said good-bye, got in my car, and left, leaving him there. All alone.

At the time I didn't think too much about this man. But now, looking back, I think he was more than an ordinary man. Let me explain.

The word 'angel' means 'messenger'. God sends messengers in various forms. Sometimes mortals, like ourselves, help us out, like angels. But other angels are made of fire. And others are immortal spirits, who take on human form, to serve and save those who will inherit salvation (Heb. 1.14; 13.2).

As I've thought about it over the years, I think this man was one of those. You see, everything about him was totally out of the ordinary.

First, there was just the fact that he was there. The whole depot was deserted. Not a soul in sight. Just this one man, a total stranger, standing, waiting all alone in the office. Since he was the stranger and I knew the place, he should have asked me where everyone was. But not a word.

Then there was the look in his eyes. Every time he looked at me, his eyes smiled, as if to say, "You are precious to me. I want to help you." That's not normal with someone you've never met before.

Then there was his behaviour. Your ordinary working bloke doesn't stand patiently doing nothing for twenty minutes when there's no-one around. He'll get frustrated. He'll mutter or swear. He'll walk off. But this man waited in perfect peace.

And there was his silence. I don't remember him saying a single word to me. But he didn't need to. His look and his smile said everything.

And he saved me from deadly peril when cruel men sought my blood. Isn't that what angels do?

So over the years, I concluded that this man was an angel sent to help me. One day, I hope to meet him again and thank him. But now I know that the Father sent his angel to deliver me from evil.

After all, what good is a God that cannot deliver us from evil?

24. But What If He Doesn't?

B UT THERE'S a flip side to this. Let's not hide
from it. What if we pray to be delivered
from evil, yet evil still hits us?

Of course, it's like this with all our prayers for
ourselves. We may pray for our daily bread, but not
get all we want. We may pray not to be led into
temptation, but still face trials. So we may pray to
be delivered from evil, but evil still comes.

We must accept we won't be saved from every
evil, because some are sent by God. Death is the
best example. No one can cheat death. Not me. Not
you. Not the World Heavyweight Boxing champ.
Death is our lot. It's God's judgement on our father
Adam's sin in the Garden of Eden (Gen. 3:19).

Nor can we avoid getting older as we approach
death. Old age brings weakness and often sickness.
We won't be shielded from all these things. They
are also part of God's judgement on Adam.

Nor can we avoid hard work. That too comes
from God's judgement (Gen. 3:17).

But what about other things. Things that are not
inevitable. Like the miscarriage of a long-awaited
baby. Or the sickness or death of a little one. Or
betrayal and divorce. Or accident. Or war.

In all these things, we must accept again that God is in charge. He tells us to pray to be delivered from evil. And we should pray, just as he tells us. But, in the end, he alone decides which evils he'll spare us, and which he won't. He is God. He knows what's best. Best for us and best for others.

Some people don't understand this. They say, "How can God be good and let this happen?" "How can God be good and allow evil?"

The answer is this: Evil is part of God's good plan for a world gone wrong. You see, evils, heart-breaks, and pains are his chosen tools to restore our sanity. They break our self-confident pride. They turn us from folly. They show us we are weak and mortal. They remind us we are not in charge. They remind us that this broken, changeful world is not our Happy-Ever-After. It is a Vale of Tears we must pass through to reach the Fatherland, the Land o' the Leal, where there is no sorrow or evil or death.

Remember too that no one gets all the troubles they might get. A person may think their cup of sorrows is well filled. But they could always have more. God spares some evils to all people.

So we should pray to be delivered from evil. But we recognize that we may still see some troubles.

But I assure you of this, with all my heart. If you ask him every day to deliver you from evil, then you will see a lot less evil than if you didn't ask. Many, many troubles will pass you by.

25. *Thine is the Kingdom, the Power, and the Glory*

I SAID at the outset that the Lord's Prayer – like a sandwich – has seven petitions between the opening salutation and the closing doxology.

So now we come to the bottom slice of bread, the doxology: *For thine is the kingdom, the power, and the glory, for ever and ever. Amen.*

In a doxology, we close by giving praise to God. In doing this, we affirm that he really has the power to grant us what we have asked him for.

We begin by saying that the "kingdom" is his. When we say this, we are confessing what is really true. We are saying that, even though we live in a world gone wrong, our Father is still the true king. He is in charge. And, one day soon, he will bring in his kingdom, ruled by Jesus, the King Messiah.

We are saying that true sovereignty is his. He has full and total authority to do whatever he wants, whenever he wants, however he wants. No one can stop him. No one can rush him. He needs no one's say-so. The Father has full and total authority to answer our prayers whenever it pleases him.

Next, we say that the "power" is his. This is to remind us (if we forgot) that he is the Almighty. He can do anything. Nothing is impossible for God. With God all things are possible.

Then we say that the "glory" is his. There really is true glory, even if our world is sometimes dirty and cheap. That glory is with our Father. He is forever glorious and forever splendid.

I think one reason Jesus adds these words is to remind us to give God glory when he answers our prayers. If we ask him for success, and he brings us through, we shouldn't say, "Look at me! Look what I did!" Instead, we should give him thanks and give him glory, and say, *All we have achieved, you have done for us* (Isa. 26:12). "All was by the grace of God."

Of course, these things are true *for ever and ever.* The Father will forever be sovereign, almighty, and glorious to save.

Then we confirm all we have said with *Amen,* which is an old Hebrew word meaning 'truly' or 'certainly' or 'confirmed'.

LAST WORDS

HAPPY FOR EVER

26. Happy For Ever

THIS BOOK is about how the Lord's Prayer can make you happy for ever. Let's revisit the road we came to see how it can do that.

Our Father in heaven. When we begin to pray these words from our heart, we get ourselves a new Father. A Father Almighty, All-seeing, All-Present, and Eternal; a Father loyal and never-giving-up. And we get a big brother, the Lord Jesus, the King Messiah, who died for the sins of the world, and rose again, and is coming back to rule. And we get a new family, the Father's children who confess the name of Jesus, scattered through every country on the face of the globe.

Hallowed be your Name. With these words, we shake off the darkness of our egotism and we begin to praise God. When we do this, the power of God flows into our soul. For God blesses everyone who blesses him.

Your kingdom come. When we say these words, we confess that the Father is going to bring a beautiful new kingdom into our world, ruled by the Lord Jesus. And, saying these words, we show that we want to be part of that kingdom. And so he will keep us a place in that kingdom.

Your will be done on earth as in heaven. When we say these words, God will show us his will, so we can do his will in the world. By doing this, we please the Father, and we live in his blessing, and we bless other people.

Give us this day our daily bread. When we say these words, the Father will provide all we need, every day we say it.

Forgive us our debts as we also forgive our debtors. When we say these words, and forgive those who have done us wrong, then the Father will forgive us the wrongs we have done. That way, we will live before him accepted and clean.

Lead us not into temptation. When we say these words, the Father will protect us from situations where we will be tested beyond what we can bear. He will save us from the fiery trial coming upon the world. He will save us from the Day of Judgement.

But deliver us from evil. When we say these words, the Father will deliver us – our body, our mind, our soul, our spirit, our loved ones –from the devil and all evil. He will protect us and set his shield around us, by day and by night.

For thine is the kingdom, the power, and the glory, for ever and ever. Amen. We close, just as we began, by confessing and praising the Father's kingship, power, and glory. He blesses those who bless him.

27. Objection, Your Honour

SO NOW we've looked at the Lord's Prayer together. And, like I said, if you say it every day you'll be happy for ever.

Yet some folk don't like me talking this way. They say I'm making the Lord's Prayer into a magic formula. They imagine that I'm saying you can believe anything you like, and you can behave any way you like, but you'll be blessed as long as you mindlessly parrot the Lord's Prayer every day.

But I'm not saying that. Just show me where I ever said that!

Right behaviour and right belief are important. But if you say the Lord's Prayer every day, then right behaviour and right belief will follow. By saying this prayer, you fulfil a direct instruction of Jesus. Following his command is the gateway to blessing. The knowledge of God will enter your life. It will set your feet on the road of discipleship. That road leads to eternal happiness.

As for praying the Our Father mindlessly, that's not likely, is it? After all, you know what the words mean, don't you? It's not in some long-lost tongue like Pictish or Tupi. If you didn't agree with the words, you wouldn't say them, now would you?

Imagine someone came and told you to pray every day, "O God, I beg you to turn me into a dirty little cockroach that feeds on a dunghill."

You wouldn't pray that prayer, would you? Obviously not. You don't agree with that prayer.

It's because you agree with the words of the Our Father that you say it every day. And yes, of course, it's best to say it mindfully. But how often are we ever 100% mindful? The Lord understands our busy lives. So just say it every day, the best you can. He will bless your obedience.

Back in Chapter One, I said that this book is about what the Lord's Prayer can do to make *you* happy. Some might say I'm putting the cart before the horse. Isn't the Christian life about *us* doing what God says, not about God doing what *we* say?

That's true. But most of us come to the Lord first because of our own needs. In the gospels, folk come to Jesus when they are blind, lame, deaf, dumb, or sick. Jesus helps them. It's only later they tell him, "Lord, I'll follow you wherever you go."

Remember, we are dealing with our Father. He wants to help us. He also wants us to obey him. His help and our obedience go hand in hand.

Let me sum it up like this. If you pray the Lord's prayer every day, you'll be a true disciple of Jesus. And all his true disciples are happy for ever.

Now three more things to close: Bible, sharing, and community.

28. The Bible

THE BIBLE is the most wonderful book in the world, the most precious thing on earth. It's the fount of all wisdom. It's a magic hospital where you go in blind and come out seeing. It makes the foolish wise. It's the heart and soul of true Christian faith. This is because it speaks the living words of the living Spirit of the living God. Whoever loves and reads the Bible becomes filled with holy wisdom. Whoever doesn't, stays empty.

Yet in some ways, it's very strange. This book began when the pyramids were new. It's newest bit is from Roman times. It records words and deeds of ancient people in a small corner of the ancient world. Yet, in these far-off words and deeds, God has recorded his revelation to the whole world. (Well, if you were God, how would you do it?)

That's why the Bible is as new as your next breath. It answers our daily questions. It teaches us right from wrong. It is God's holy law to guide our feet through his world. It would set our world right if only people would read it and believe it.

There's no such thing as a real Christian who doesn't read the Bible. Jesus knew the Bible inside out. Leave it closed and you'll never be more than a half-Christian, fooled by every false teaching. But read it and you will see with the eyes of God.

Long ago, you couldn't read the Bible. Its manuscripts were kept in sealed treasuries and seen only a few times a year. When printing was invented, it was the first book to be printed. Yet it still cost a year's wages. And it was in Latin, which most folk didn't know. And most folk couldn't read anyway. Too bad.

But folk began to translate it, even at the cost of their lives. Bit by bit, Bibles began to appear in languages people could read. But they were still expensive. You had to be rich to own a Bible.

But, over the years, they got cheaper. And now, everyone, everywhere, has instant free access to the Bible on the internet. Never before has it been so easy to read. And never before has it been so widely ignored. When it was hard to read, folk honoured it but didn't know it. Now it's easy to read, they ignore it and mock those who love it.

But you, pray to become a person who knows the Bible. Pray to understand it. It will make you happy, wise, and perfect. It will be your key to the promises of God, your map to the Land o' the Leal.

Read it every day. Read it all. From Genesis to Revelation. Then start again. Read three chapters a day, and it will take a year. Better still, read it in parallel, Old and New Testament every day. Or read it any way you like. Just read it.

29. Sharing

NOW WE have come to know the Father, now his goodness has touched our lives, it's normal to share it with those we love. Share it first with your own family. If you have children, begin with them. You want them to grow up with the blessing of heaven, don't you?

Moses tells the people of Israel:

These words that I instruct you today are to be on your hearts. Make your children repeat them. Speak of them when you sit at home and when you walk on the road, when you lie down and rise up. (Deut. 6:6–7)

The book of Proverbs promises that a child brought up this way will remain walking in the truth.

Train up a child in the way he should go,
And when he is old he will not depart from it. (22:6)

Some Christian parents think it's the church's job to teach their children faith. That's a big mistake. Even if the youth ministry in your church is good, they get your kids only for a little while each week.

The duty of bringing up your children in the faith lies with you, the parent. It's you who must teach them how to read the Bible and pray.

If they're young, it's easy. Sit them down and read the Bible. You can start with a kids' Bible. Read a passage together. Talk about it. Pray the Our Father. Then add any special requests of your own.

You can do this first thing in the morning, before school and work. Or do it in the evening, before they go to bed. Don't say it's too hard. Being happy for ever depends on this, for them and for you. It's more important than anything. It's way more important than TV. So make sure you do it.

But maybe you say, "It's too late. My kids are grown. They're not interested in the Bible."

Why do you say it's too late?

Begin by saying to them, "Can we read the Bible together?"

If they say "No," then you say, "Well, can we just pray the Our Father together?"

If they still say, "No," then say, "Well, how about I say the Our Father for you, and you listen?"

If they still say, "No," then you say, "Well, I'll pray for you even if you don't listen." Then place a hand on their arm or head and pray the Our Father.

If they walk off, continue your prayer. Do this every day until they stay and listen. Then continue every day until they join in. Then continue every day until they listen to the Bible. And keep this up for as long as they live under your roof.

But what if they've already left home and are wilful and faithless. In that case, phone them up, once a week, and repeat the conversation above. Then pray for them over the phone. If they hang up, finish your prayer, and repeat the process on the same day next week. Every week.

I know a couple who brought up their children with the Bible and prayer from the womb. When they were babies, they read a kid's Bible to them every evening. This went on for ten years. Then they decided to read the Bible evening *and* morning.

Every morning, they read between them a chapter of Proverbs and a short Old Testament passage. Then they prayed the Lord's Prayer.

Every evening, they read a Psalm between them, then usually a New Testament passage. They gave reasons for being thankful. Then they prayed, not forgetting the Lord's Prayer.

Morning prayer is good. You commit the day's tasks and concerns to heaven and pray for safety. Evening prayer is good too. It comforts our hearts with God's presence before we sleep.

With these folk, it took about ten minutes every morning and fifteen minutes every evening. Some evenings it took a bit longer. But it was mostly a fun time, with jokes and laughs at the day's events, and memories from long ago. It wasn't just a time of prayer, but a time of family sharing.

Twice a day may seem a lot. It needs discipline. But here's the truth. This couple had no trouble with these kids. And they are very proud of them.

These folk aren't perfect. They had plenty spats. But those who pray together, stay together. And they're still together. God set a shield around that family and those young people. And it's still there.

Me, my parents loved the Lord. They read the Bible and prayed with me till I was about seven. But then they said, "You're old enough to say your own prayers now." But I think they gave up too soon. Left to myself, I didn't pray or read the Bible on my own. My child-like faith in God faded. Maybe that's one reason why I became a teenage ne'er-do-well.

So, father or mother, never give up praying with your children. Never. From the day they are born till the day death parts you.

There's a passage I love by the Maronite poet, Khalil Gibran. It's based on Psalm 127. He says:

You are the bows from which your children as living
   arrows are sent forth.
The Archer sees the mark upon the path of the infinite,
   and He bends you with His might that His arrows
   may go swift and far.
Let your bending in the Archer's hand be for gladness;
For even as he loves the arrow that flies, so He loves
   also the bow that is stable.

Be a steady bow that shoots your arrows straight into the future. Not wiggly arrows. Not bendy or broken arrows. For the Heavenly Archer loves the steady bow and the straight arrow. Make your kids fly straight. Let them be your shining gift, your bright blessing, to the world.

But what about folk apart from your kids? If you're trying to reach an unbelieving husband or wife, then follow pretty much the same process as for your children. Ask to pray with them. If they refuse, just pray for them every day. The day may come when they will soften and join in. Persist.

If it's a friend or a work colleague, then be a bit gentler. But the time may come when they have a trouble or a problem. Then you can say, "Why don't you pray the Our Father?"

They'll maybe say, "How is that going to help me?" Then you can say, "Why don't you try?" You can offer to pray with them, if that's your style.

Our towns and cities are full of folk who are anxious and distraught. But you, now you have found the Father, you know he can help them. But how can you tell them? You must simply shine a light in all the little ways you can.

One way is just by saying, "God bless you." If someone helps you in some small way: "God bless you." If a neighbour gives you a cake, "Thanks, Caroline. God bless you."

Years ago, when I was about nineteen, I went into town with my little cousin, Joy. We got on the bus. She asked the driver to tell us when we were at the right stop. As we drew near the stop, we moved to the front of the bus. Then the driver leaned round and said to Joy, "This is your stop now, love."

He opened the doors. She smiled and said, "God bless you." Easy as that. Just three words.

Those three words hit me hard. Yes, I thought it was twee. But there was something lovely about it. I felt, "I'd like to have that kind of light in me." Maybe the bus driver felt the same way. And I suppose God did bless him, just like she said. And, over the years, those three words touched me too.

So these days, I say "God bless you," to people when I can. Maybe it sounds twee. But when you say "God bless you" to someone, there's a big chance that God will do just that. And if that person rejects your blessing – if he curls his lip and says, "There is no God" – then your blessing will come back to you. So it's a good thing to say any time.

Sharing your faith needn't be difficult or tough. If someone tells you the world's a mess, then say, "Maybe the Lord is coming soon." In the old days, people used to preach in the market place. But these days, the market place is online. So share the good news on your social media page, or write a blog. Or if none of that is your style, just name your friends before the Father and ask him to bless them.

You could even speak to them with a gift. You could get them a cute little book about being happy for ever. With a bright amber cover. Maybe a bit like this one. And fill in their name on the first page, where it says "A Gift For..."

30. Community

BACK IN Chapter 9, I said that now we are the Father's children we should meet up with our brothers and sisters.

Jesus did this. He used to worship together with the people in his local synagogue every Shabbat day, once a week (Luke 4:16). A synagogue service had Bible readings, prayers, songs, teaching, and words of encouragement. A bit like a church.

Later, the first Christians met once a week. These meetings were quite like the synagogue, but they also shared the Lord's supper.[11] In the same way, we also meet together every week, to encourage one another, and to learn, and pray, and praise together.

So ask the Lord to help you find a good church where the pastor or priest is a decent person who believes the Bible. And then become part of that Christian community.

If you've not been baptized, you should be baptized. In the New Testament, it's an important mark of being a Christian (Mark 16:16).

In the New Testament, people were always baptized by full immersion, totally under the water. But some early Christians lived in the Egyptian or Syrian deserts. Water was scarce. So they baptized by affusion – pouring water over the head. Some folk took this further and thought it was enough to just sprinkle some water on the head.

Nowadays, many churches still sprinkle. But others – Baptists and Pentecostals – baptize only by full immersion.

Of course, churches also vary on whether you should be baptized as a baby or an adult.

The reasoning for baptizing babies is that God welcomes the children of Christian parents into his family of faith. That's surely true.

The reasoning for baptizing adult believers is that a person should make a conscious profession of faith before being baptized. That is surely best.

Some early church fathers reached a compromise by baptizing children around the age of three. At that age, a child can believe in God and make a personal profession of faith. That seems to me like a good solution. But it never really caught on.

Is there an answer? Well, the New Testament has no clear teaching on the subject. When the gospel was new, most people were baptized as believing adults. But there were also family baptisms which probably included children (Acts 16:33).

But if you're being baptized for the first time, as an adult, there's no issue. Just get yourself baptized. Since New Testament baptisms are by immersion, then that's the best way to do it, unless you live in a desert.

31. Turn Your Life Around

RIGHT AT the beginning of this book, I said that the really important thing is to *say* the Lord's Prayer, not study it.

Yet I wrote this little book to encourage you. And you've read it. And I hope it has helped you to see how saying the Lord's Prayer can change your life.

But now it's time to stop reading and start doing.

Resolve in your heart. Tell yourself, "From this day on I will try to say the Our Father every day." Keep saying it and see what blessings it brings.

With this power in your corner, you can start to tackle things in your life that you long to change.

Change begins with hope. Everyone needs hope. We need it like water or air. Without hope, people perish. But you, now you have hope. You have a Father Almighty on your side. You can start to turn your life around.

There are three steps to doing this.

First, **identify** the things in your life that you want to change. Is it lack of money? Or loneliness? Or over-weight? Sadness? Addiction? Anger? Family break-up?

Second, **believe** that things can be better. Say to yourself, "This problem doesn't have to be permanent. It can change." Another voice will say, "You can't change. You're trapped." But you have an Almighty Father on your side. So thank him that he is with you. Ask him to help you see the answer, and the way to achieve it. This might also be a good time to ask the advice of a good friend.

Third, *act*. It is your own action, together with God's help, that can change your situation. So write down what you will do. You may need to find many pathways to achieve your goal. Maybe you need to write letters. Maybe you must invite folk for coffee. Maybe you should join a support group. Or go to evening classes. Or keep a journal of your drinking. Or stop going to certain places. Identify as many pathways as you can. And act on them.

Whatever good thing you resolve to do, your Father will be there to help you. Don't expect all the changes to happen overnight. Some changes can take decades. But don't give up. *Omnia perseverando vinces.* (The persevering one conquers all things.) Keep trying to go the way that looks best to you. But if you find a door continually shut in your face, ask if God is pointing you in another direction.

You – yes, you! – can still make something good and beautiful of your life. You can even change the world. But you don't have to change it from the top down, like politicians and ideologues try to do. You can change it from the roots up, by helping the folk around you, like Jesus did.

Find an honest job, and do it honestly. Do the things you should be doing, the things that other folk are counting on you to do. Bring up your family in the teaching of the Lord. Live at peace with your neighbour. If everybody did these things, the world would be perfect.

Don't seek to be number one. Be willing to live humbly. Yet don't give up your dreams and ambitions! They are your road-map to the future. One day, what you achieve may bless the world. Begin by setting yourself attainable goals. Then work and pray to see your goals become reality, one by one. Step by step, you'll see progress. And don't forget the adage: "If you want to change the world, start by making your bed." Do these things and transform your own corner of the world.

Say the Our Father daily from your heart. It will bring untold blessing on you and your loved ones. Like the fruitful rain from heaven, blessings will descend on your heads. Heaven will smile on you, provide for you, protect you, and make your paths straight. Blessing will flow out to your wider family and friends, way out beyond what you can see.

Jesus died and rose to give us pardon, power, and life. The Our Father is the key to this treasure. It is the forgotten power of the disciples of Jesus. It's the nuclear option that does good, not harm. It will generate light and power and success and blessing and happiness in our societies. It has power to melt mountains. It has power to change hearts.

But evil must remain for a little while. For the wheat and weeds must grow together until the harvest (Matt. 13:30). But until that day, this prayer will be a shield around you. Then the Lord Jesus will be revealed from heaven in blazing fire. He will raise the dead, and unite his people in the kingdom that we have prayed to come. We'll walk together in the Father's promised green pastures. And we'll be happy for ever.

I'm hoping to see you there.

Notes

1. This is the version of the Lord's prayer that we see in the old Revised Standard Version. It's a bit old-fashioned. But it's still the one that many folk know best. It's also the one still said at events like weddings or funerals or Armistice Day or Christmas services. But you can use any version you like. The main differences are "Forgive us our debts/trespasses/sins" and "Lead us not into temptation/trial". More on these later.

2. The song is by Carolina Nairne (1766–1845). In modern English it would be:

   I'm wearing away, John,
   Like snow-wreaths in thaw, John,
   I'm wearing away to the Land of the Loyal.
   There's no sorrow there, John,
   There's neither cold nor care, John,
   The day is always fair in the Land of the Loyal.

3. That means,

   So dry your tearful eyes, John,
   This world's cares are vain, John,
   We'll meet and be happy for ever in the Land of the Loyal.

4. From the last verse of *Leanabh an àibh* by the Gaelic poetess Màiri Macdonald of Bunessan.

5. The earliest Christian text after the New Testament is *The Lord's Teaching Through the Twelve Apostles to the Nations*. (It's often called by its Greek title, *Didachê*, or "Teaching".) It was written by the disciples of the apostles near the end of the first century AD. As its name says, they wrote it so all nations would know what Jesus taught the apostles. Its main concern is how Christians should practise their faith. It quotes the Lord's Prayer (§2). Then it says, "Pray thus three times a day." From this we can see the apostles taught the first Christians of the Holy Land to pray the Lord's prayer three times a day.

6. For Tetiana's story: https://edition.cnn.com/2023/02/22/europe/ bucha-ukraine-russian-occupation-rebuilding-intl/ index.html

7. The declaration that "nothing is impossible for God" is found

all through the Bible. The Lord said it to Abraham and Jeremiah (Gen. 18:14; Jer. 32:27). The angel Gabriel said it to Mary (Luke 1:37). Jesus said it to his disciples (Matt. 19:26).

8. I should add two riders here. First, we find the name 'Yah' 48 times in the Old Testament. It's found mostly in the Psalms, and mostly in the phrase 'Halelu Yah' (Praise Yah). It is a contraction of 'Yehovah', just like Pippa is short for Philippa or Wim for Willem. It's really the same name.

   There is one other name which is half-title and half-name. That is Immanuel, which means "God-with-us". It's a name revealed to the prophet Isaiah for the coming Messiah. We find it only three times in the Bible (Isaiah 7:14; 8:10; Matthew 1:23).

9. Some say the name is actually Yahweh. A German theologian called Gesenius proposed this, and another German theologian called Ewald made it popular. But there is no evidence for this pronunciation. The best Hebrew text of the Bible (the Aleppo Codex) says *Yehovah* all through. If you want to know more, see Appendix I in my book *The Songs of Ascents.*

10. In fact, the name Yeshua is basically the same name as Joshua, who was Moses's assistant, back around 1400 BC. (His name in Hebrew is Y'hoshua.) He led the Israelites into the Promised Land. And in some ways he is like a picture of the Messiah who was to come. In time, his name (Y'hoshua) was contracted to Yeshua, the name of Jesus. But they are still really the same name, with the same meaning: *Jehovah saves.*

11. See Acts 20:7; 1 Cor. 16:2; Heb. 10:25.

We hope you enjoyed this book.
If it helped you, we'd love to hear about it.
Honest reviews help people find books that help them

Manufactured by Amazon.ca
Acheson, AB

12871312R00062